Peg Quinn's poems in *Mother Lode* are songs that pull you "like a sturdy hand toward the dance floor" that is her life. They embrace the earthiness of Nebraska fields where her childhood is "planted," the holiness of nature where a barn is a "cathedral," the ocean a place of "worship," and death in its sorrow or horror, a "reckoning." She writes with a grace and voice uniquely hers. I found myself bowing after each poem.

—Perie Longo, Santa Barbara Poet Laureate Emerita

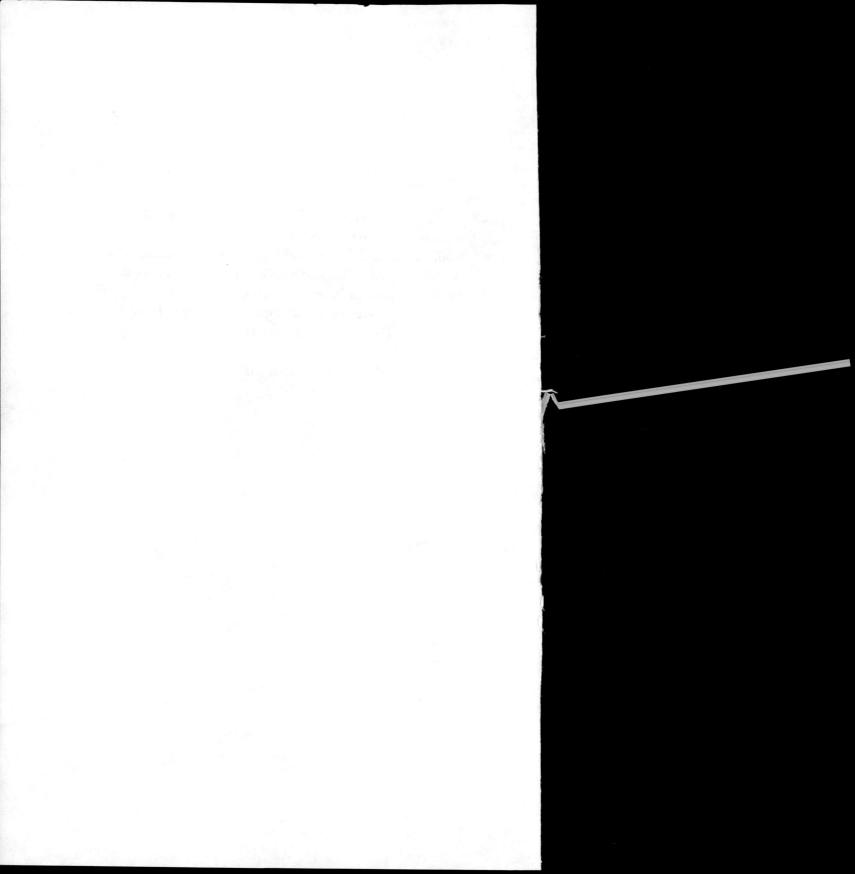

MOTHER LODE

POEMS

PEG QUINN

GUNPOWDER PRESS • SANTA BARBARA
2021

Published by Gunpowder Press
David Starkey, Editor
PO Box 60035
Santa Barbara, CA 93160-0035

Cover Illustration: Peg Quinn

ISBN-13: 978-0-9986458-6-5

www.gunpowderpress.com

For Anna and Alex with love,
and gratitude for everything you've taught me

ACKNOWLEDGEMENTS

Many thanks to the editors of the following publications in which these poems first appeared, sometimes in slightly altered versions:

ASKEW: "More Stories from Nebraska Life, *Nebraska Life Magazine* Will Never Publish," "Someone's Sons," "Ferris Wheel" and "Blue Collar Pickup"

Bubble Magazine: "Today's News and Weather"

Calliope: "Nesting Season"

Edible Ojai: "Ode to a Pear" and "How to Bake Cookies"

Green Poet Press: "The Crow's Calling"

Malibu Surfside: "Redemption"

Miramar: "To the Family of a Vietnamese Man Killed in a Boat on an Unknown River, 1965" and "Back in Nebraska"

Nebraska Life Magazine: "Cautious Horses Eyed Us," "Who Decides" and "Spring Planting"

Negative Capability Press: "Hero"

Origami Poems Project: "Gardening," "To the Creator of Random Beauty" and "Blood Moon"

Poor Soul's Press: "When Girls Go Fishing" and "Mangos"

Rattle: "When the Buddha Farmed Nebraska"

Sage Trail: "Leaving the Bar"

Salt: "Mother Lode"

Spillway: "By the Light of the Moon"

"Someone's Sons" won the 2018 Ventura County Arts Council and Poet Laureate Committee's contest on the topic of Californians.

CONTENTS

I.

II.

III.

I.

*"What lies behind us and what lies before us
are small matters compared to what lies within us."*

—*Ralph Waldo Emerson*

Someone's Sons

Glancing in his rearview mirror
the foreman cracks a beer, floors his
monster truck and roars away
leaving two illegal boys on their knees
above my steaming driveway,
filling cracks with bottled blacktop.

I bring them paper masks, simple
borders between toxic dust and
young, well-traveled lungs,
hand them cans of coconut water.

Earlier, I'd read a message from my son,
rear-ended by a motorcycle last night
on the Hollywood Freeway,
everyone pulled over,
first-responders there in minutes—
no one seriously injured.

I bring the boys dark, juicy plums.
Something sweet for someone's sons.

SoCal Illegals

Rain washed out the gardeners' morning.
They've gathered beyond my back door,
oblivious, leaning on trucks, getting soaked,
laughter muffled, except for one high-pitched
trill - like a girl. I smile, embarrassed for him.

They're dressed in layers of faded clothes,
teeth framed in gold, defiant knuckles raw,
determined as their letters home.

When the sun returns, they'll protect their necks
with bandanas draped from baseball caps,
scrunch into dented trucks and clank away
to guaranteed uncertainty.

Blue Collar Pickup

Hey, ladies fans, can we fall in love?
You fit with me like a boxing glove.
   —rapper Ill Mitch

Country Night, *Creekside Inn,*
Dancing Begins at Seven.

Two strangers' hands neatly cup as they fumble
in a slow two-step, he presses the flesh of her back,
she reaches up for his shoulder.

He towers over, content to hold
her so soft/otherworldly/womanly body
if only for one dance,
so when she leans back in a nervous laugh,
he calmly pulls her in, keeping steady rhythm,
closing his weary eyes when their bodies finally
synchronize.

Now quick-quick-slow is the only ritual they
need to know, and that after a long, lousy day
following bosses' orders, she smells of soap
and lets him lead.

Come. Party.

for Robin Gauss

At Ontare, turn toward the mountains.
The street will narrow to a single lane of gravel.
You'll know you've left the city when
a red-tailed hawk soars from its nest.

The road ends at the iron gate leading to
Robin's ranch, with pigs and dogs, submarine
parts, ocean bottom ploughs, motorcycles,
a bulldozer, hospice for horses, a cantina
with a stage, a bar and a fireplace, elephant
tusks, bison skulls, and a black and white
of Marilyn Monroe.

Yesterday, the road washed out in three places
when rain loosened walls of earth from the mountain,
destabilizing today's plan to surprise Robin with
a party on his 70th birthday.

This morning, when Joe's old gold
station wagon pulled up, we all walked out
to greet him - assuming he'd found a new location -
but he didn't smile, just said, *Robin's dead.*

Robin's dead.
Last night his wild, abundant heart gave out.
It's chaos, but the road was cleared, and today
we will celebrate Robin's birthday.
Bring the beer and cake and candles.

Come. Party.

A Note of Thanks

Honey, get it while you can.
  —*Janis Joplin*

A well-kept black Buick crept through the parking lot
as if time no longer mattered, eventually found a spot,
and cautiously, came to a stop.

Thank you, elderly man in hip denim jacket and worn
baseball cap, who creaked in slow motion around the back
to the passenger's side to aid a small woman,
her one daring toe touching pavement.

Thank you, stylish high heel with striped sock,
frail and waiting.

Thank you, practiced precision.
With arms gently clutched,
he eased her up.

When steady, she held him with the wide smile of love,
while arranging a too-large sweater.

Oh, thank you, smile and tangled clothes.

He leaned down low, eyes closed.
Even their kiss was long and slow.
Thank you.

To My Student Who Jumped Off the Cold Springs Bridge

I stare at the evening paper.
Suffocate on emotion.
Stare out the window.
A dependable lone palm
towering steadfast against
endless sky.

You were only eighteen,
tumbling from my field of reason.
Numb with grief now,
though I barely knew you.

In 6th grade, you were tall, quiet,
helpful. The one I could trust
to set an example.
At twelve you seemed more man
than boy.

Sunday, you left the world behind.

You'll be forever falling in my mind.

And There's This

After lunch, the kindergarten playground
is wild as the modern world.
Body-to-body, kids cyclone down spiraling
slides, squealing, swinging, a monkey's paradise.

From a patient tree, a murder of crows caw
a raucous, wild applause, eager to attack food scraps
under picnic tables.

While the thin, special-needs girl stands alone
on the side, too frail and confused to join in,
until Isaac, her gifted friend, spots her.

His laughter sobers as he elbows his way out of line,
gently takes her hand, turns sideways, watching her
feet so she won't stumble, as if escorting a partner
in stilettos onto the dance floor.

Guided by him to the jungle gym, she's welcomed in,
quiet, smiling, eyes widening, hair blowing,
now one of the tribe, finally,
flying.

Nesting Season

for Chris

In a nested dent of drain pipe
swaying above the library door
a wren is calling his mate—

silent, she waits,
toes curled on the edge
of the garden gate,
before singing her reply.

When we met for lunch,
you smelled of pine.

I watched you flirt with the girl
behind the counter,
as she nervously refolded
perfectly-folded napkins.

Disproving the Data

Research advises
we shut blinds tight
when sleeping,
as brightness creates
depression in mice.

Yet, late that night,
I woke to the moon
gilding the curves
of your body,
spawning such pleasure,
we moved from moonlight
to regions
science can't measure.

After *Taming the Shrew*

for Joe Tower

Taming the shrew, Petruchio
throws a chair across the room,
pounds the table,
flips it over, striking angst
in front-row theater goers
fearing his anger

When the play is over,
he exits the stage door,
shoulders curled, fists in pockets,
dark eyes sweeping shadows
cast by his frayed, hooded jacket.

He turns toward the boulevard,
to be swept by the tide
of wide-eyed tourists
surging the sidewalks,
music festooning from every door,
shoppers clutching purses,
their pictures taken
with boa constrictors,
Darth Vader, or Marilyn—
her glamor eternal.

He's oblivious.

Fixed on his lines.
Rehearsing his monologue,
skull full of Shakespeare.
As he nears the bus stop,
the content of his brain
remains more dazzling than
all the neon signs in Hollywood.

To the Family of a Vietnamese Man Killed in His Boat on an Unknown River, 1965

Dear long-grieving family,
your father, son, brother, uncle
still screams from the heart of his killer.

Was he fishing that day,
or wiring water mines?
Doesn't matter.
Our young, numb helicopter pilot
was obeying orders when his
rat-a-tat-tat shattered his target,

gripping his soul with a grief
that won't unravel.

Fifty years later, he trembles
when telling the story,
and your father, son, brother, uncle
lives again,
his dreams floating
in bloody water, and we
want to go back,
rewrite the day,
let him arrive home smiling
with a catfish catch for dinner,
because our young numb soldier
was looking over his other shoulder

and will get to grow old with simple,
ordinary, explainable regrets.

Hero

for Uncle Bob

This night, easing back in bed,
morphine soothing his system,
he revisits the Great Depression,

walking to school through snow
without a coat,
in shoes that don't match,
he drifts

to Guam,
his tank under fire,
slow motion of body parts in water,
the gunner's beheading,
crimes never mentioned
until his wife's death,
sixty years later.

Somewhere
there's a box of medals.

Now, his mind turns bedside,
his infant son,
polio,
the good man he would become.

His wife's smile warms the room.

He smiles back,

remembers owning the sky
in their Piper Cub,
tandem seating,
their carnival of friends,
Ferris wheels of laughter,
his good fortune,

the landscape of his life
a clean horizon.

This night,
straining through pain
between tabs of morphine,
he finds the faded Navajo rug bought
from the back of a pickup truck,
their honeymoon stop near Santa Fe.
The light in the eyes of his spunky bride
that night under stars.

Tossing the rug on the floor of the garage,
he drops down hard,
hugs his gun,
pulls the trigger.

Sea Glass

for Christine at mid-life

The fortunate journey here,
find themselves
burnished and bare,
used,
smooth, where once
broken,
better for wear,
casting bright shadows;

whole altars
to impermanence.

Redemption

Though another refugee boat
is overturning, Allepo burning,
planet warming, future blurring,

I'm driving the smooth
Malibu curve as a deep orange
resting sun dazzles cloudy puffs
into peach and pink.

Light bounces down on waves
stretched to the edge of the world,

while boulders and sandy cliffs
sink to dark silhouettes,
bearing witness with such reverence,
the heavy fog of human failure lifts.

Every Death a Reckoning

for Jackson Wheeler

Learning of your passing swept me
into Death's country, where I
do not speak the language,
though the clatter of everyday living
flows past like water around
my solid stone of emptiness.

And the wind, howling through trees
or maybe
trees, crying in the wind.

Doors and windows rattle, and though
I'm of no man-made religion, it is silence
and a clear bell ringing I need.
I long for ritual, like sitting shiva.

You gone.
Everyone in the room but you.

Or, your presence fills the room.

The world transformed,
your absence a vacuum,
your voice silenced.

Or, your voice a steady whisper.

Late Night on the Dance Floor

As the shrunken,
faded couple
shuffle slowly,
cheek-to-cheek,
oblivious to the beat,
inching their way
around the edge
of the sawdust floor

their history is written
in the imagination
of a smiling crowd,

romance waltzing thick
as blue barroom smoke,

they don't notice
the band packing up,
just snuggle closer,
dancing, forever,
in the kingdom
of together.

Volunteering at the Homeless Shelter

Awakened by wind searing trees
like the whine of a witch missing teeth.

Savored rain with a toast of hot drinks,
poems, morning paper, while streams
rose to the edges of gutters.

Took a hot shower, soap, bubbles
slathered lavender lotion.

Crossed town through dark morning,
branches littered streets.

At the homeless shelter, the line had
been forming for hours,
gray garbage bags of stuff cozied up
to gray garbage bags of rain cover.
Weathered, ragged faces stared,
ready for lunch.

Parked. Sat in my car.
Listened to the growing whistle
of a slowing train.

Sunday at the Supermarket

for Kenny

A casual glance at blue sky
out the plate glass window
and, without warning,
your death surrounds me.

Two weeks after you died, Dad said,
It's time things got back to normal.

Fifty years later, I'm shoved out of time,
trying not to cry on a sunny day
at the supermarket, pleading with Death
to grant you a pardon. Begging it never happened.
That you didn't fade, daily, in indifferent
cotton, tiny blinking lights counting down
your departure.

And if my plea is honored?

We'll drive down gravel roads to the ice cream
stand, wedged on the edge of a dairy farm—
me, vanilla bean; you, chocolate.
We'll trade for a taste, and when your scoop
plops from its cone onto my lap?
We'll live forever in that laugh.

Field Notes

I study your mouth as you talk.
It's asymmetric, one eye-tooth
leaning slightly back.
Your smile, too, a bit askew
stretching so wide,
I move closer.

When your mouth finds mine
lips/tongues/search/soft
determined—
I know you know
exactly what you're doing,

so when I clasp my hands around
your neck—next step in your
practiced recklessness—
you undress us both, our
bodies then, not our own but
one emotion melding flesh
beyond the reach of notes, time,
logic...

... as we recover, inspecting
the new-found magic of each other,
I study your mouth as you talk,
one eyetooth leaning slightly back.

Things I'll Miss

Sheets, waving
from the clothesline,
drunk on sunshine,
finally stretched
across my bed,
their surgical precision
welcoming sleep.

Next morning,
I sit beside my steaming
cup of coffee,
smoothed
with milk and honey

while songs from the radio
pull like a sturdy hand
toward the day's dance floor.

Notes for an Oil Painting

Driving south to L.A., colors fade,
as yawning light drenches the landscape.

Greens recede to grays.

Rounding a curve, a row of taillights
defines the side of a mountain.

A silver train, tilting, strains the track,
rumbling past.

While the distant city glows hills into
flat shadows as we speed into night's
dark palette.

II.

". . . and bowing, not knowing to what."

—*W. S. Merwin*

Mother Lode

Leave wallet, phone and
garbled emotions in your car.
Pocket keys.

Turn to the black, mulched path,
winding through a young field
of newly-minted grass.

Horse's hooves pressed in moist dirt
symbolize good luck.

Sandpipers assembled on the beach,
turn in unison, face the ocean,
eye its surface.

Lessons lie in patterns:
abalone, obsidian,
a broken chambered nautilus.

Down the bluff, in silhouette,
a row of surfers walk,
boards balanced on heads,
granting assurance—
you've entered the right place
of worship.

Idle God's Thunder Storm

The lumbering ocean
slowly rose
like an idle god
who knows no measure
of restraint.

Waves crashed,
a muffled avalanche
of white froth, flying
like a dancer's petticoats,
while the stones
being herded
down the shore
snapped as they rolled
like breaking bones.

Above the distant mountains,
rumbling clouds
climbed and crowded,
debating how to best
the water's grandeur.

Then the sky fell dark
before a dirge of thunder.

The Crow's Calling

A black hole
shaped like a crow
was strutting a path across
bright playground grass
before rising,
leisurely,
at an angle

to observe from the perch
of a stark eucalyptus,

to caw forth a sermon,
determined,
inspired as a priest on
a foreign mission,

ignoring the fact
of our language difference.

Ode to a Pear

So yellow, it penetrated
through gray morning haze,
surprising me with a request
to *please pay attention!*

So I stopped.

Felt its weight in my hand.

Noticed its rosy blush, as if
the sun had warmed its rump
to perfection.

Then I took in
its flesh, its juicy candor,
biting small chunks
of light.

Moon Shadows

Moon splatters dancing shadows
of leaves on an indifferent, empty
black parking lot. Shadows dancing
like they own the night.

I'll drive home slowly tonight.

Grateful ...

... that the coffee shop I've ignored for months
is open when I desperately need it, a motorcycle cop
with all his gadgets doing paperwork outside on a picnic table,
reminiscing on the Northridge earthquake with a guy
barely awake ...

... that walking there, I saw at the bar across the street
the shaved head, tattooed bus driver emerge with a broom,
the bus driver who on karaoke night sobers the room with a voice
that should have made him famous,
grateful that he's sweeping here, in my poem ...

... that my teenage son phoned from his road trip to ask
how was my day in court, then brought me a souvenir
yellow plastic duck-head lunchbox with protruding bill,
a gift to the me stuck at age six ...

... that my former mother-in-law, who I met when I was ten
is bringing salads for lunch, in order to see the bureau I'm painting,
commissioned to include all the flora and fauna of the Sierras on its
surface, and I did ...

... grateful that she and I agree on everything, except the death penalty ...

... that school will be starting soon, its petty politics
playing out like a Bingo game ...

... that in *Our Town*, Emily asks,
Do any human beings ever realize life while they live it?

... that I know my stay is limited, that I will vanish one day,
my constellation of atoms scattered, yet mysteriously
remain, when in the future, my son then bent and gray,
buys his six-year-old granddaughter a yellow plastic duck-
head lunchbox, not remembering why.

While Gulls Circle

Rain ignored overflowing
grass and gutters,
draped an old wool
blanket of sky,
too close and heavy.

At the beach
confused waves
break north,
mud-brown and
bottom heavy,
heaving themselves
in surrender
toward shore.

Debris scatters
across soggy sand
like a shattered dream
while in their patient,
ancient ritual,
gulls circle.

Christmas Day

Kids flown to the East Coast
so I take a short drive
to Coal Oil Point, climb over
a wooden fence, slide down the cliff,
find my balance when I hit
firm sand left by morning tide,
then realize at my feet lies a rugged,
blue, sea glass heart.
I pick it up, look around, no one here,
miles to myself.
As I slowly walk toward the point
where the cliff takes a dramatic curve,
I hear a lonesome trumpet wailing.
Two young men wearing knit caps with
ear flaps stand, the other holds
a sax. Smiling, I stroll up, ask if they
take requests? They're German, don't
speak English, but get my drift, manage,
What you like?

From nowhere I ask,
I Can't Help Falling in Love with You?
They stare at each other, shake heads
and frown. I add, *Elvis Presley?*
Enthusiastic nods, *You sing?*

I do: Wise men say, only fools rush in ...
We laugh. I give up, *danke schön,*
turn away, then, maybe forty beats later,
they play it. Slow.

Like swelling waves,
Like a river flows, surely to the sea.

And I walk, waves tugging rocks, steam rising up.
I walk to a trumpet-sax-Elvis Presley-
love-song-sound-track before I see someone
was here before me—
a crooked word: HEAVEN, carved in sand.

Who Decides

Who decides when seagulls rise—
their pop and snap of pressing wings
a celebration?

Commuter's Ode to a Pear Tree in a Thunderstorm

With branches raised
in resplendent surrender, you
welcome the storm's rough touch
on your rain-blacked trunk.

Blissfully ravaged by wind,
your celebration
casts a blesséd mess
of white petals
cloaking the ground below,

transforming this dark morning
at a glance.

Leaving the Bar

The moon surprises,
flash bulb bright,
the air a cool splash
after cramped bodies,
muted roar of the party,
urban games demanding
more of my brain than
tipsy neurons allow.

I stand in the doorway,
silent moon, pool balls crash,
raucous bar, ancient rock,
feel their dazzling differences

'til the moon, my chaperone,
sees me home.

Mangos

I ate two mangos for breakfast
while standing over the kitchen sink,
peeling, slicing, thinking how
objects of nature face their fate
without complaint.
Then,
how the color mango differs from
say, apricot, becoming clown-like,
dripping mango mess
while consumed by the idea
that sacrifice is so complex
we've conjured whole religions
in an effort to make sense.

Crossing

While walking
a vast constellation
of sea debris, my other
loves pale compared
to this jewel-shadowed,
wave-swept, perfection.

Notice light passing
through you,
through the waves,
through the stones.

Three dark women
sit watching
silent, solid where
they're perched
here at death's border,
life's border,
death's border.
Feel it breathing.

Don't be afraid.
Cross through the veil
into the light.
Come back again
to dark matter.

You need the practice.

Blood Moon

I don't know where the moon will rise tonight,
or exactly when, but the Bridge to Nowhere
is lined with cars as I approach the edge of
a mountain, the curious and eager in
lawn chairs or adjusting cameras as

a peach sunset trumpets its crescendo;
the sky curls over in a gray blanket,
allowing stars access to night's stage,
while lights lining the ridge of the mesa
sparkle in celebration, and

we stand,
an ardent tribe of strangers,
breathing night air, and awe
then,
silence
as the red moon rises.

I lose my balance, teetering
between science and magic.

To the Creator of Random Beauty

Thank you for dropping by.

The black crow assessing the blustering mess
of red leaves against a storm-tossed sky
was a reassuring sign.

Dark Matter

Balanced like solid notes
on the swaying tip of a lone Star Pine,
in silhouette against gray sky,
two crows redefine dark matter.

The *London Times* Ran an Obituary on the Death of Common Sense

the same day a family of longlegs completed
their evolution high in the corner of my
shower. The male, off-stage, watched
with due diligence as the nearly
invisible, milky buds
surrounding his patient mate
blossomed
into a
constellation
of tiny,
falling stars,
rappelling
from the
ceiling,
their skills
exceeding
reason.

Today's News and Weather

Trees toss, content in the force of elements.

Cars and boats float in a tsunami, news so fresh,
it streams faster than the studio tech can insert
a meaningful soundtrack.

Then a letter waltzes in,
your symphony on berry season,
stained hands straining for the shaded cluster,
one arm pressed against a wooden fence,

while outside my window, a crow
apparently in audition for the role
of nightwatchman, struts,
indifferent to roiling events, unable
to do anything but play his part
to perfection.

III.

"Most of the material a writer works with is acquired before the age of fifteen."

—*Willa Cather*

When the Buddha Farmed Nebraska

Grandpa emanated Buddha-nature,
yet I doubt he'd heard the phrase.

He gave thanks after hitting his
thumb with a hammer, and when
he shot milk from the cow's teat
toward the cat's open mouth,
he never missed, smiling,
Thank you.

Thank you, to the sloshing
bucket of milk, to the mud riding
up his galoshes.
He sang,
through tornadoes and harvests,
Thank you.

Faith

Our stampede down the dirt path
stopped at the silence.
Nothing so solemn to a small child
as a still barn.

We entered the cathedral as dust
filtered through shafts of light,
and nervous swallows
darted through rafters.

A ladder rose two stories
to a four-by-four beam.
The bale rope, our swing.
Bare feet gripped one knot,
hands clutched another.

Like a pendulum, we'd sail,
waiting for the will to let go,
to fall,
simply fall,
out of thought,
out of time,
to be caught
by the fresh,
waiting
wheat.

When Girls Go Fishing

They rise in the night
before earthworms,
blind to their fate,
squirm in the bait pail.

Walk alone past
darkened houses,
down gravel roads,
through dew-wet woods,
to arrive at the creek
as day breaks,
cast lines, and wait.

Mid-morning,
stripped to bathing suits
and supervised by
dragonflies,
they cross the creek,
their voices drowned
in wild applause
of rushing water striking
rocks,
as moss floats like
mermaid tresses,
and catfish glide.

They lie on the bank
and nearly doze
cross back, repack,
and head for home.

Cautious Horses Eyed Us

Great-Uncle Ed said if we
could grab one of the carp
swimming in the horse tank
down by the barn,
we could take it home.

With sleeves rolled to our shoulders,
arms dangling in cold water,
bodies baking in the sun,
cautious horses eyed us.

As we justified details of how
the last one got away,
an enormous, indifferent fish
eased up from the depths
just out of reach.

We'd spring for the catch,
brushing just a slip of life
as it moved past,
leaving us thrilled
by the feel of
an empty grasp.

Letter to Grandma

Ruby,
I want to take the loose skin
of your worn face between my hands
with the pressing need of a faith-healer.

We, the seeds of your silence,
sit empty, watching the worn path
you walk once more into the kitchen.

Hot coffee will not warm us.
We await your serving up
the rich warm delicacies
your unspoken words deny us.
You keep them sealed away,
airtight.

A frail fragile woman holds
three generations on ice.
While like an indifferent child
poking dollhouse furniture,
she rearranges for us stale
pastries on a plate.

Preparation for Cemetery Maintenance, Rural Nebraska

Plant perennials, rows of pink peonies
before the first frost.
Line your driveway.
Blooming through late Spring
they'll survive until Memorial Day.

Clear your calendar for the third week in May.
Saturday, serve a standard farmer's breakfast:
eggs, oatmeal, toast, homemade jam, ham,
juice, and coffee with too much sugar.

Coordinate breakfast cleanup with picnic packing:
canned beets, potato salad, cold chicken, baked beans,
heat-and-serve rolls (unheated), iced tea with
too much sugar, and Lemon Velvet Cake using the
recipe that earned your Blue Ribbon at the County Fair.

Plastic plates and tumblers will do
but *please*, utensils must be stainless steel.
Bring food for six times the number in your party—
you never know who might show.

This would be a good time to pull on a pair of
lightweight, knee length shorts, however, if you've
never worn anything but a housedress and apron,
don't bother to change. Men—today is the reason for
overalls, paint-splattered shoes and old hats.

Your son will arrive with his truck.
Load it with lawnmowers, picnic baskets, peony bouquets

held in foil-wrapped coffee cans, rakes and gloves.
Pick up grandchildren on your way out of town.

Drive thirty miles from the highway to gravel roads.
Pass the weathered farms where you spent your youth.
Retell stories.
The truck will lurch when passing through the cemetery gate.
Children will squeal, as covered dishes and peonies go
sliding to their peril. Park in the shade.

As you use your hand to sweep dry leaves from family
headstones, the day grows suddenly solemn. Listen.
The eternal wind is moving across the plains.
Granddad will remove his hat before reciting a verse by heart.
(Study his face. His eyes will be closed.)

Remember me as you pass by
As you are now, so once was I
As I am now, soon you will be
So prepare for death and eternity

Allow for a brief, awkward silence before assigning tasks.
Make sure everyone has the tools they need to proceed.

Painting the Cemetery Fence

Grandma
in housedress
and apron,
hair blown a mess,
ruining her first pair
of canvas shoes,
every surface
splattered with
whitewash,
clutching a brush
with both hands,
painting the
picket fence
surrounding
the cemetery,
Nebraska
circa 1955,
laughing,
befuddled,
never
seemed
more alive.

Back in Nebraska

for my brother

February,
and this world is frozen.

I kneel at your grave,
brush away snow,
trace your name with
a mittened finger.

Stare at your stone.
Stare at black, jagged
skeleton trees.

Sit in brittle silence,
listening,
as the gray sky
leans closer.

Pig's Population Control

We were finishing lunch
around the dining room table
when Howard shouted
from the barn.
We shoved our chairs in unison
and ran. Sows were circling
the yard—a cyclone pattern—
packed tight, bellies bumping,
closing in on the weakest one
to solve their need for
larger quarters.

With short legs splayed,
the runt stood braced,
mouth agape, eyes rolled open,
tongue frozen as it screamed
and waited.

Wendell marched in with a club,
gripped by flashbacks of the time
his friend had slipped, and was
mauled to death.

Howard strained with the heavy gate
allowing swine some extra space,
yet each required an extra shove
before grunting away.

A Pale Pink Death

I was four years old,
dawdling around the back
of the pasture, then stepped
into a scene of butchery.

A hog was hanging upside down
from the branch of a tree,
dainty pointed hoofs crossed
like a ballet dancer's, then bound,
body stretched and sagging.

I stood watching.

My first impression
was the incongruity
between its exquisitely looming
pale pink death,
and my handsome grandfather,
and my handsome uncle, lean
and sunbaked, standing nearby
in belted jeans, telling stories
and laughing, sometimes glancing
at the heavy body,

then glancing at me.
Said they were "draining blood,"
then went back to chatting.
I liked bacon and knew
where it came from.
Never thought about how
the throat was sliced, gaping open,
blood gushing out like a faucet,
pooling in a perfect circle.

More Childhood Stories from Nebraska Life
Nebraska Life Magazine Would Never Publish

Our three-room school house in rural Nebraska lay on a stretch of prairie dubbed "Tornado Alley." I loved the curtains running the length of the room for their pattern of cowboys on bucking broncos. Bravo to whoever made *that* decision!

One day, Mrs. Mason, kindergarten-first-and-second-grade teacher was tugging at the drapes, yelling, *There's a tornado coming—everyone under your desks!* Like we'd practiced in the event of a nuclear bomb. But from where I stood at the back of the room, the sky was clear and blue, and I was torn between logic and terror before noticing Mrs. Kanjinski, sitting on a tree stump in her yard next to the playground, crushing a handkerchief, weeping. I slid under my desk and held on.

Truth was, eighth grader Johnny Jansen, always in trouble, had once again left the playground to run through the cornfield behind the baseball diamond— which was forbidden.

The same Johnny Jansen who would die three years later when a rifle blast ripped through the back of his head. His best friend accidentally pulled the trigger, having forgotten to unload his gun after hunting pheasants.

Which reminds me of Russ Riley—smart-ass, tight pants, motorcycle madman with cigarettes cuffed in the sleeve of his tee. A James Dean wanna-be nobody liked, until a four-by-six beam fell from the barn loft smack on his head. Then he walked the edge of gravel roads, pudgy and waving.

And my ten year old friend Joey, who cut off four fingers with a power saw. It was a long, winding drive to the city, but he didn't feel pain for the first twenty minutes.

But back to Bobby. Fortunately, or unfortunately, he'd tripped on the body of Mrs. Kanjinski's fourteen year old daughter who'd taken her dad's gun to the cornfield, having put two and two together and realized she was pregnant.

Lying under my desk, trying to remember all the words to Buddy Holly's, "Peggy Sue," I didn't notice when another teacher told Mrs. Mason the sheriff and ambulance were on their way.

I guess she thought we were slow learners, using the tornado spoof a few weeks later when Charles Starkweather, our home-grown killer, was spotted in his car, heading our way.

Gardening

once more, for my brother

The morning sun rests on my shoulders
as I bend in a row of white flowers plucking
wilted blossoms, thinking of you, more than
forty years since you faded in a bed of
fresh white sheets and pillows.

When I'm even less than what comes after
scattered ashes—you'll still matter.

High School Formal

After the Winter Formal,
after we'd paid our dues,
cooed over glittering streamers
drapping the auditorium,
politely sipped punch from glass cups ...

After we slow danced - bodies separated
by unspoken etiquette and the stern
stare of chaperones ...

After greeting our geometry teacher,
the principal, and our frowning advisor
who would go to her grave a luckless virgin ...

we hustled out into a snow storm
collapsing, at last, in the padded interior
of a borrowed convertible, reeking
of possibility.

We took Highway 77 to meet friends
at a dance hall in Denton, but first
parked on the narrow airport service road,
headlights bouncing off falling snow,
to stare in silence at the stream of blue lights
lining the runway.

Then Tom turned up the music.

We danced in white drifts, noses warmed
on each other's faces. We danced to the beat

of our desperate breathing
then roared off through the glistening storm
with the top down, blasting the heater
as the blizzard went crazy—
unable to reach us.

By the Light of the Moon

I.

At sixteen,
sneaking after curfew,
I'd step over
the creaking third step
on the stairwell,
slowly creeping
toward the back door,
boyfriend waiting
in his car
down our gravel road,
engine purring
taillights gleaming.
He'd bring wet bottles
of Coca Cola.

II.

News trickled in ...
A war in Vietnam,
he phoned one night
from Fort Benning,
shipping out
next morning,
thought we should
get married, his
voice trembling.

I said we'd talk
when he got back,

never dreaming
his final flight
in a body bag.

III.

Now, decades later,
I check the night sky
before going inside,
Orion, Pleiades,
Cassiopeia,
the Universe in order.

Then the moon appears,
arriving late in earth's
spinning orbit,
waking me
through an open window,
beckoning.

How to Bake Holiday Cookies

Light candles.
Pour wine. Admire the color,
the distance traveled.
Check your heart for bitterness.

Adjust accordingly.

Gather ingredients:
brown spices and sugar,
molasses, flour, lard, eggs, and salt.

Pile them onto the counter.
Celebrate their reunion.

Phone your sister.
Feel her fears through the phone,
her brokenness. Make her laugh.
Remind her of the Iowa blizzard,
when you baked deep into the night.
Remember the mess, the hilarity.

Start mixing.
Listen to the sounds of your children
converging on the kitchen,
never too grown-up for cookie dough.

Watch their faces.
The past and future dance across them.
Adjust your heart accordingly.

Roll dough into ropes, then cut into small pieces.
This takes time, and tiny cookies bake quickly
so pay attention.

As they bake, you wait alone, remembering
your grandmother, her calico aprons
and braided hair, her quiet efficiency.

Muse on your daughter,
her purple glittered nails
and eyeliner.

The kitchen is warm and fragrant.
Candles flicker.

Your job is done. This is the ritual.
Adjust your heart accordingly.

Ferris Wheel

One lucky ride, your seat creaks to the top.
The entire contraption groans to a stop—
someone's turn to get off—
and you're instantly lost in details
of the now miniature carnival,

distant city lights, fields, farms,
trees snaking the river, until your eyes rest
at the rim of the sunset.

On cue, stars move from behind evening's
deepening curtain, their patterns perfect,
while your seat swings like a cradle,
rocking the world.

Spring Planting

Let dirt fall endlessly
through your fingers
like you did when
innocent of the world's
complications
Slowly fill your lungs
with earth's rich scent.
Plow a furrow curved
to contain the will of water

Marry seeds in ritual pairs,
pushing earth firm
to secure their future

Praise the symphony
of sunlight
listen, part of you
is planted here, too
feel your future taking root
as you walk the splattered shade
of blooming dogwood
back to the rest of your life

AUTHOR'S NOTE

My gratitude to the following, whose guidance, support and encouragement
brought me here:

Carol DeCanio Abeles, Tom Bouse, Chris Buckley, Ann Buxie,
Marsha De La O, Dan Gerber, Kurt Goerwitz, Friday Gretchen,
Richard Jarrette, Ken Jones, Jan Keough, Lois Klein, Greg Kuzma,
Dan Ladley, Peri Longo, Enid Osborn, Ellen Reich, Rita Shaw, Barry
Spacks, Chris Spangenberg, David Starkey, Phil Taggart, Paul Willis,
Jackson Wheeler and Chryss Yost

ABOUT THE POET

Peg Quinn grew up in rural Nebraska. She has a B.F.A. in Education from the University of Nebraska, Lincoln. Her poetry and creative nonfiction have been published in numerous journals and anthologies and nominated three times for the Pushcart Prize. She lives in Santa Barbara, California, where she is an educator and visual artist.

Barry Spacks Poetry Prize Series

2015
Instead of Sadness
Catherine Abbey Hodges

2016
Burning Down Disneyland
Kurt Olsson

2017
Posthumous Noon
Aaron Baker

2018
The Ghosts of Lost Animals
Michelle Bonczek Evory

2019
Drinking with O'Hara
Glenn Freeman

2020
Curriculum
Meghan Dunn

Also from Gunpowder Press

The Tarnation of Faust: Poems by David Case

Mouth & Fruit: Poems by Chryss Yost

Shaping Water: Poems by Barry Spacks

Original Face: Poems by Jim Peterson

What Breathes Us: Santa Barbara Poets Laureate, 2005-2015
Edited by David Starkey

Unfinished City: Poems by Nan Cohen

Raft of Days: Poems by Catherine Abbey Hodges

and the Shoreline Voices Projects:

Buzz: Poets Respond to SWARM
Edited by Nancy Gifford and Chryss Yost

Rare Feathers: Poems on Birds & Art
Edited by Nancy Gifford, Chryss Yost, and George Yatchisin

To Give Life a Shape: Poems Inspired by the Santa Barbara Museum of Art
Edited by David Starkey and Chryss Yost

CPSIA information can be obtained
at www.ICGtesting.com
Printed in the USA
LVHW091001160121
676459LV00008B/487